J
613.7
KOO

 P9-DEY-349

WITHDRAWN

Manteno Public Library District
50 West Division
Manteno, Illinois 60950-1554

TAI CHI
FOR FUN!

by Robin Koontz

Content Adviser: Sifu David Chang, Head Instructor, Wushu Central, Santa Clara, California
Reading Adviser: Frances J. Bonacci, Ed.D, Reading Specialist, Cambridge, Massachusetts

Compass Point Books ✦ Minneapolis, Minnesota

Compass Point Books
3109 West 50th Street, #115
Minneapolis, MN 55410

Visit Compass Point Books on the Internet at www.compasspointbooks.com
or e-mail your request to custserv@compasspointbooks.com

Photographs ©: David Chang, front cover (left), 19, 21, 22–23, 25 (left), 26, 27, 28–29, 30, 32–33, 34, 39 (right), 43 (all), 44 (bottom); Alex Bramwell/iStockphoto, front cover (right); The Image Works/Topfoto, 4–5; Simon Krzic/BigStockPhoto, 5 (top); Digital Vision, 6 (all); The Travel Library/Rex Features, 6–7; Jari Bilen/ BigStockPhoto, 8; UPP/Topfoto, 9; Heribert Welschenbach/iStockphoto, 10 (front); The Image Source/Rex Features, 10–11, 47; Ulrike Hammerich/iStockphoto, 12, 45; Rick Donovan/iStockphoto, 14, 16 (left), 44 (right); Charles Walker/Topfoto, 15; Shane Partridge/Rex Features, 16–17; Anness Publishing, 18, 25 (right), 31, 35; Keren Su/China Span/Sunset/Rex Features, 36–37; Topfoto, 38–39; Chris Ronneseth/iStockphoto, 40, 42; Everett Collection/Rex Features, 41; Stephen Solomon, 44 (top).

Illustrator: Jon Davis
Editors: Lionel Bender and Brenda Haugen
Designer: Bill SMITH STUDIO
Page Production: Ben White and Ashlee Schultz
Photo Researcher: Suzanne O'Farrell
Art Director: Jaime Martens
Creative Director: Keith Griffin
Editorial Director: Nick Healy
Managing Editor: Catherine Neitge
Tai Chi for Fun! was produced for Compass Point Books by Bender Richardson White, UK

Tai Chi information based on "A Simpler 8-Form Easy Tai Chi for elderly persons," by Fuzhong Li, K. John Fisher, Peter Harmer, and Machiko Shirai, *Journal of Aging and Physical Activity*, Vol. 11, 2003, pp. 217–229.

Library of Congress Cataloging-in-Publication Data
Koontz, Robin Michal.
  Tai chi for fun! / by Robin Koontz.
     p. cm. — (For fun)
  ISBN-13: 978-0-7565-3288-8 (library binding)
  ISBN-10: 0-7565-3288-4 (library binding)
1. Tai chi for children—Juvenile lilterature. I. Title. II. Series.
  GV504.6.C44K66 2008
  613.7′148083—dc22   2007004898

Copyright © 2008 by Compass Point Books
All rights reserved. No part of this book may be reproduced without written permission from the publisher. The publisher takes no responsibility for the use of any of the materials or methods described in this book, nor for the products thereof. Printed in the United States of America.

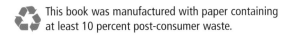 This book was manufactured with paper containing at least 10 percent post-consumer waste.

Table of Contents

The Basics

Doing It

People, Places, and Fun

Note: In this book, there are two kinds of vocabulary words. Tai Chi Words to Know are words specific to tai chi. They are defined on page 46. Other Words to Know are helpful words that aren't related only to tai chi. They are defined on page 47.

Tai Chi

A small group of people gathers outside in the early morning. They move their arms, legs, and bodies slowly. It looks like they are dancing in slow motion, but there is no music. They seem very calm and peaceful. What's going on? They are practicing tai chi.

Tai chi is a type of martial art that began in China many centuries ago. It is now practiced all over the world. Tai chi teaches both inner peace and outer strength. It also teaches balance, flexibility, and agility.

Tai chi is a series of postures or poses that are done together in a smooth, unbroken movement. There are many styles of tai chi. The style of tai chi discussed in this book can be practiced as a form of exercise.

People of all ages and levels of fitness can perform these gentle exercises. Many people who begin to learn tai chi practice it for the rest of their lives. They might also teach others, just as it was taught in years past.

Why learn tai chi? It can inspire creativity, relieve stress, and increase balance and coordination. It's also a fun way to exercise!

Tai chi (pronounced tie chee) is short for tai chi chaun, which in Chinese means "supreme ultimate boxing." At first it was used for self-defense. Tai chi is best learned from a teacher, but a book is a good start!

Learning From the Animals

Nobody really knows who invented tai chi. One story is that a healer who lived in the third century believed that people needed exercise. It would help with digesting food and blood circulation. The healer taught the movements of the tiger, deer, bear, ape, and bird. Copying the movements of these animals would help people exercise every joint in the body.

Another story credits the start of tai chi to the Chen family, which had been teaching many kinds of martial arts since the 16th century. In the 17th century, Chen Wang-ting created new ways of fighting. He was in the Chinese military and had studied boxing methods, too.

Telling History

Much of tai chi history is not written. Instead the history was told to the children in the village. As the children grew up and left home, they took tai chi with them.

There is also the story of Chang San-feng, who was thought to have been born in 1247. This Taoist monk lived alone in the mountains and worked on a new fighting style. He had a vision in which a crane tried to attack a snake. Each time the crane stabbed at the snake's head, the snake got out of the way and slapped the crane with its tail. When the crane tried to stab the snake's tail, the snake would bite the crane.

These methods of dodging and attacking are the basic ideas of tai chi. This book will show you how they are done.

The Eternal Contest

The word *chi* means universal energy. It is the energy that is part of all life. Chi is the center of the tai chi way to good health and well-being. You can have more energy by practicing tai chi.

Tai chi can be shown with the yin yang symbol. This is taken from the Chinese philosophy, Taoism, which believes in the natural way, or path, of life. The yin yang symbol looks like two fish chasing in a circle. The yin fish is dark and the yang fish is light.

Their chase shows the relationship between two opposites. Examples of yin and yang are night and day, and winter and summer. Though yin and yang are opposites, they hold each other in balance. Day follows night, and winter flows into summer.

Self Defense
Tai chi, as exercise or self-defense, teaches you to react with balance and relaxation.

Traditionally Chinese medicine has aimed to restore energy balance and chi using the practices of acupuncture, acupressure, exercise, massage, and herbal medicine. Herbal remedies, breathing, and the use of exercise for good health go back more than 4,000 years.

Why Tai Chi?

What kind of exercise do you do? Walking is good. So is playing basketball or volleyball. How about something new and different—something you can do indoors or out? How about something you can do with someone or alone—without any special equipment or clothing? That's tai chi!

Through the years tai chi has developed into many different styles. The five most common styles are called Yang, Chen, Wu, Sun, and Woo. They are named for the families who created them. All the styles show differences in posture, stance, and movement. Each style is different, but all styles have the ideas of tai chi in common.

Those who practice tai chi learn to tune in to their bodies. But they don't just close their eyes and shut out the world. They remain aware of their surroundings. They are also aware of their bodies and minds. They relax and are at peace, yet they feel powerful and full of energy.

Some people practice tai chi in the morning before starting their day. And often they practice again before going to bed. In the morning it can help them prepare for the day, improving focus and energy. In the evening it can help them relax before sleep.

Tai Chi Outdoors

Practicing outdoors helps bring you in tune with nature as well as yourself.

11

The 13 Postures

Tai chi consists of 13 basic postures. There are eight positions and five directions. In tai chi, you want to send energy in a direction where it cannot be harmful to your body. This is done using the 13 postures.

Tai Chi Postures

The 13 postures are also known as the 13 powers or energies of tai chi.

The five directions of tai chi involve precise footwork and legwork.

Forward Movement is the front foot placed on its heel. Then as your body moves forward, the toes are placed. **Backward Movement** is stepping backward with your toe first, then heel. **Movement to the Left** is rolling to the left on one foot. **Movement to the Right** is rolling to the right on one foot. **Settling at the Center** is centering and standing balanced.

The eight positions mostly involve the arms and hands:

Ward Off is a response to incoming energy. The goal is to bounce energy back like a big rubber ball. **Pull Back** is the second posture. You interrupt the energy and move it to one side.

Press is pressing and receiving energy. **Push** is downward pushing energy. **Pull Down** is grabbing energy and pulling. **Splitting** is striking energy that splits apart an opponent. **Elbow** is striking energy that uses elbows. **Shoulder** is full body striking energy. It is delivered with your shoulder or back. Football players know this movement well!

A String of Pearls

Tai chi is made up of moves that use combinations of the 13 postures. Each move has a name, such as "Grasp the Sparrow's Tail" or "Repulse the Monkey." These names are translated from the Chinese language. They describe the postures used to complete a move.

A tai chi form is a combination of movements of the body. Each form has a beginning and an end. Each move in the form is like a pearl on a string. All of the moves are connected so that they flow easily into a progression. One form of tai chi can have 118 moves!

What is the speed of moves in tai chi? There are no rules. The goal is to feel calm and in control. The slower you move, the more energy you get. Make the shift from one move to the next a smooth action. Stay alert and aware. The names of each move hint to what comes next.

Chinese Tai Chi

The Chinese National Sports Committee wanted to popularize tai chi. The committee asked four tai chi experts to create a short form that would be easier to learn, remember, and practice. In 1956 they created the 24 Simplified Form based on the Yang style of tai chi.

Take a Deep Breath

No special clothing or shoes are needed to practice tai chi. There are no uniforms.

Clothing should be loose to allow for free movement and deep breathing. It should also be static-free. Cotton works well. Avoid wearing tight pants or clothing that will make you perspire. Shoes should be comfortable—and waterproof if you practice outside in wet grass in the morning.

Connecting movements and completing a form is not easy unless you are relaxed and centered. You need a place to relax! Set aside a special time just for you. Pick a place that makes you feel good. Maybe it's a quiet room with no distracting clutter. You might have a special place outside, such as a park or a playground. You might like soft lighting or music. You'll probably want to turn off the TV and the phone.

Before you begin, listen to your breathing. How many breaths do you take in a minute? Eight to 12 times is average. There are no rules. Just breathe in a natural way. Find your rhythm. You will find that it feels right to exhale during the projecting movements, such as Push and Press. It will also feel natural to inhale during movements like Rollback and Pull. Always breathe gently and quietly.

Get Ready

Tai chi is not difficult once you are ready. Do some relaxing exercises before you start. They will help loosen up your body. Stand with your feet placed below your shoulders. Relax your shoulders. Roll them forward and backward together, then one at a time. Next tilt your head gently from side to side. Your back and neck should feel loose, not tense. Gently roll your head in a circle, first left, then right.

You should not lock your elbows or knees. They should also stay relaxed.

Let your arms hang loosely. Pretend there is a thread attached to the top of your head that goes to the ceiling. Pretend the thread is pulling you up, and relax your spine.

Now find your center of gravity. In tai chi your center is just below your navel and inward, toward your spine. That spot is called dan tien. Concentrate your breath and your weight there. Let yourself sink and feel rooted to the ground. Relax your hands; there are no clenched fists. Breathe gently.

You are ready to begin. You will always want to feel this relaxed as you practice tai chi. When you bend your knee, keep your knee over your toes, not in front of your toes. Always sink your weight-bearing leg before stepping. Keep moving, and never lunge into a movement.

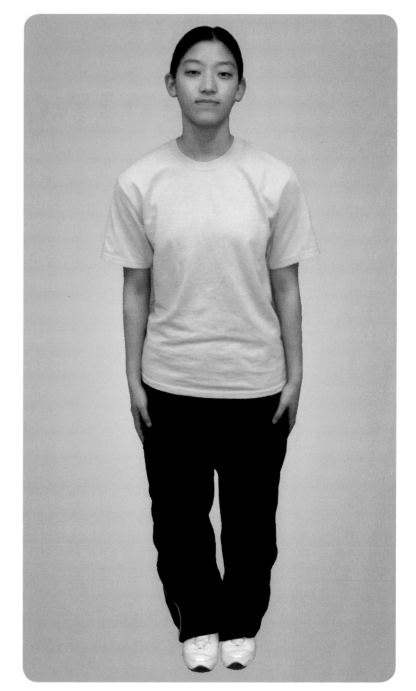

Opening Form

Let's begin. Your feet are together with both knees unlocked. Your arms are at your sides. Face forward. Your weight shifts to the right. Open your left leg to shoulder width apart. Your toes point forward, and your arms hang alongside your body. Your eyes look straight ahead.

Extend your fingertips, and slowly raise your arms up, elbows unlocked. Bring your arms to shoulder level with your palms facing downward. Slightly lower both arms while bending your legs. This leads into the next movement.

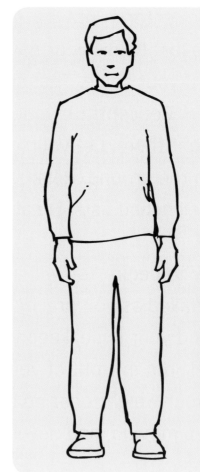

Position 1
As you move your feet apart, focus forward and keep relaxed.

Position 2

Raise your arms, and bend your legs.

Manteno Public Library District
50 West Division
Manteno, Illinois 60950-1554

Repulse the Monkey

Move your right hand downward in a semicircle until it is level with your right shoulder. Your left wrist twists so the palm faces up like you are holding a ball. At the same time, shift your body weight to the right foot. Remember, move slowly and purposefully.

Now push your right hand forward with your body weight shifting to the left side. At the same time, lower your left arm downward in a semicircle until it is level with your left shoulder. Your left palm faces up. Your right wrist twists so the palm faces up like you are holding a ball. Repeat twice on each side. Now you are ready for the next movement.

Position 1
Opening position

Position 2
Pushing forward

It's Just Human Nature

In Chinese mythology, the monkey represents human nature that is usually good but sometimes is tempted to misbehave. Repulse the Monkey implies retreating and waiting for the right time to move, rather than using force against force.

Grasp the Sparrow's Tail 1

Turn your left foot away from the middle of your body toward the left side. Then turn your upper body 90 degrees to the left. Move your left hand forward, arriving at chest level while pressing your right hand down to the side of the right hip. This completes the ward off position.

A 90-degree angle is one-fourth, or a quarter, of a full circle.

Turn your upper body slightly to the left while moving your right hand forward to almost meet your extended left hand. Pull your hands down in a curve past your stomach, until your right hand is extended sideways at shoulder level. Your elbow should be bent upward. Your hands then join in front of your chest. This completes the pull back position. You are now set up for the next posture.

Smoothing the Bird

Pressing one hand down is like smoothing the bird's tail while the other hand grasps the bird's head. The bird is a symbol of air, spirit, and breath.

Grasp the Sparrow's Tail 2

With your weight seated on the (rear) right foot, pull both hands downward to your stomach. Push forward both hands with your shoulders relaxed and elbows dropped. This completes press. Extend both hands and palms outward and forward. This completes push.

Repeat ward off, pull back, press, and push on the right side.

Move Hands Like Clouds

Move both arms 45 degrees to the left side while you shift your weight to the left leg. Move your right hand in an arc past your face with palm facing your body. Left hand moves downward. Turn your upper body to the left with weight shifting to your left leg. At the same time, move your left hand upward with palm facing body to pass the left shoulder. Your right hand twists and starts its swing downward, palm facing the body.

Follow the direction of the left hand. Your right leg joins your left leg. Repeat this movement three times.

Fair Lady Weaves at the Shuttle

Step out 45 degrees to the left with your left foot. Your left hand moves upward to block while your right palm pushes forward and outward. Drop your right hand, and step out 45 degrees to the right. Your right hand moves upward to block while your left hand pushes forward and outward.

At all times, stay balanced and focus forward.

A Possible Origin of the Name
The name of this movement probably comes from the idea that a fair lady moves the wooden shuttle of a loom with smooth turns of her body.

Position 1

Move forward with left foot

Position 2

Move forward with right foot

Golden Cockerel Stands on One Leg

Drop your left and right hands, and slowly move your weight to your left foot. Move your right arm upward, and lift your right leg as if it is hanging from a string. Your left arm is at the side of your left thigh or hip. Return to a standing position with your feet shoulder width apart, weight evenly balanced. Repeat on the right foot.

Position 1 and 2

Drop hands, and
move onto left foot

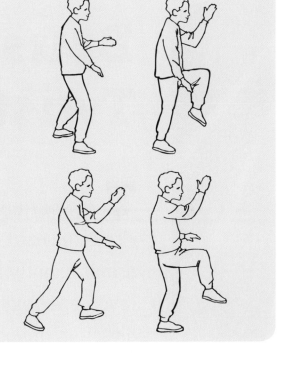

Position 3 and 4

Reverse the moves
on the right foot

Self-defense

In self-defense this is an attack
movement. One leg is raised to strike
with the knee while the other leg is
planted firmly on the ground for support.

Brush Knees and Twist Steps

Turn your upper body to the right as your right hand circles upward and outward, at about ear level. Your arm is slightly bent, and your palm faces upward (as if you are holding a violin). Your left hand follows the direction of your right hand.

Turn your upper body to the left as your left foot takes a step in a forward direction. At the same time your left hand pushes forward, passing your left knee, while your right hand pushes forward, palm facing away from your body. Repeat this for the right knee. All the time imagine you are stepping forward, pushing ahead, like a wind blowing through a forest.

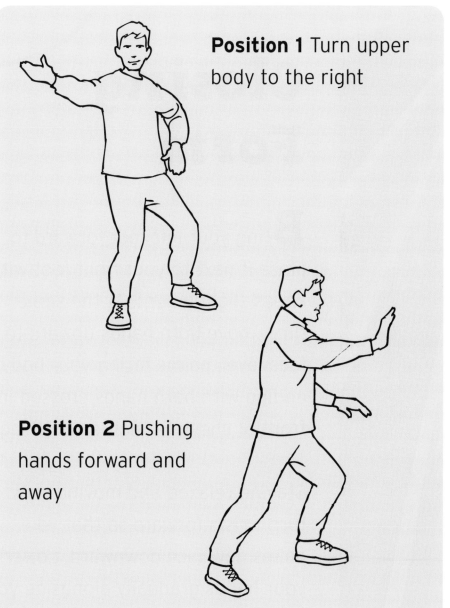

Position 1 Turn upper body to the right

Position 2 Pushing hands forward and away

Closing Form

Bring your left foot forward to place it next to your right foot with knees slightly bent. At the same time, move both hands upward to face level, palms facing your body, ending with both hands crossed in front of chest. Straighten both legs.

Staying relaxed and moving slowly, turn wrists forward so that your palms now face downward. Lower your hands gradually alongside your body. Look straight ahead.

Working Together

Push hands is a gentle way to "compete" with a tai chi partner without risking injury. You can work with a friend to improve your flexibility, balance, timing, and posture. There are lots of variations of push hands. Try several types until you and your partner find a variation with which you feel relaxed.

Tai chi is a great way to exercise with a friend.

Tai Chi Around the World

The traditional tai chi schools still focus on tai chi as a martial art. It is for self-defense as well as good health. Tai chi chaun is also called tai chi boxing. People who practice tai chi chaun use push hands, open-style fighting, and some weapons.

Other people enjoy the dramatic look and feel of tai chi. Participants dress in colorful clothing and might practice with swords or colored fans.

On the last Saturday in April, people all over the world practice tai chi at 10 in the morning. That day is called World Tai Chi and Qigong Day.

Most people practice tai chi for the energy and health benefits. They join millions in their love for the sport.

Finding a Teacher

Tai chi is one of the fastest growing fitness activities. You might find a class at the YMCA, community center, or from a private instructor. Look in the telephone book under Martial Arts.

Tai Chi Rocks

In the late 1980s the Chinese Sports Committee chose the major styles of tai chi and combined some of the forms. They wanted to take special features of each style and show them in a short amount of time.

Wushu, which means "martial art" in Chinese, is the name for a new sport that was created in China. The International Wushu Federation (IWF) holds the World Wushu Championships every two years. Wushu is both a show and a full-contact sport event. The participants compete in many different martial arts.

Tai chi, called taijiquan, is part of the competition. Participants compete in forms in all styles of tai chi. Swords are used in some competitions.

The 2008 Beijing Olympic Games Wushu Tournament will be the first wushu event in Olympic history. The IWF hopes that soon wushu will become an Olympic sport.

Tai Chi Celebrities

The sword fights in the movie *Crouching Tiger, Hidden Dragon* used many tai chi movements. Director Yuen Wo Ping also directed *The Tai Chi Master*. These movies feature martial arts including tai chi.

Lots of American celebrities practice tai chi. Famous 1970s kung fu TV star David Carradine has several tai chi DVDs. Media personality Oprah Winfrey and actor Catherine Zeta-Jones practice tai chi. They have all discovered the healthy benefits of tai chi. You can, too!

Martial arts in Chinese characters

Ziyi Zhang used tai chi movements in the movie *Crouching Tiger, Hidden Dragon*.

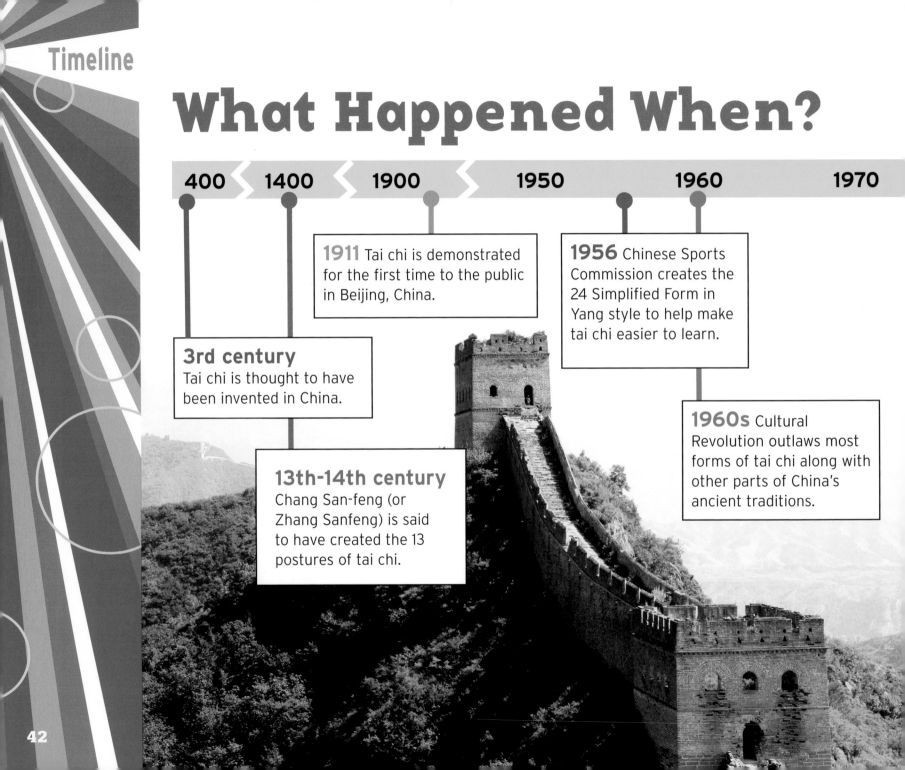

What Happened When?

400　　**1400**　　**1900**　　**1950**　　**1960**　　**1970**

1911 Tai chi is demonstrated for the first time to the public in Beijing, China.

1956 Chinese Sports Commission creates the 24 Simplified Form in Yang style to help make tai chi easier to learn.

3rd century
Tai chi is thought to have been invented in China.

1960s Cultural Revolution outlaws most forms of tai chi along with other parts of China's ancient traditions.

13th-14th century
Chang San-feng (or Zhang Sanfeng) is said to have created the 13 postures of tai chi.

| 1980 | 1985 | 1990 | 1995 | 2000 | 2005 |

1984 The first International Tai Chi and Sword Tournament is held.

1989 Competition form of tai chi is developed.

1999 The world's first Martial Arts History Museum and Cultural Center is created in California by founder Michael Matsuda.

2006 The first World Junior Wushu Championships are held in Kuala Lumpur, Malaysia.

1991 The first World Wushu Championship is held in Beijing.

2008 First ever wushu event to be held at the Summer Olympics in Beijing.

Fun Tai Chi Facts

The term tai chi was first used in about 1850. It was not until the early 1900s that many people began to learn tai chi. There are only a few brief pages of early writings about the original practice of tai chi. These writings are known as the Tai Chi Bible.

Qigong translates to energy (qi) and exercise (gong). It is a set of movements that guides qi through and around the body. Qigong forms tend to be simpler than tai chi. Many people practice both qigong and tai chi.